Aha Grammar 2

Workbook

Happy House

CoNTeNTs

Chapter 1 Nouns & Articles

Chapter 2 Pronouns

Chapter 3 Present Simple Tense

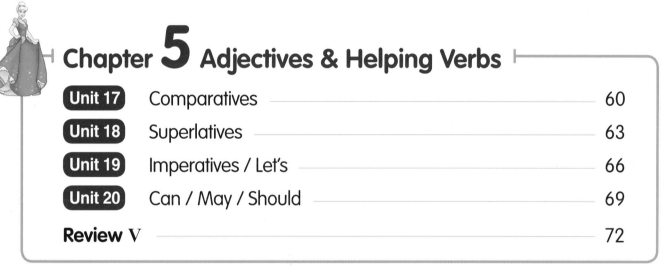

Regular Plural Nouns

GRAMMAR POINT

복수명사 (규칙변화)

● 복수명사는 사람, 장소, 동물, 사물 등이 둘 이상임을 나타내며, 단수형에 –s나 –es를 붙여 복수형으로 만드는 것을 규칙변화라고 합니다.

① 대부분의 명사는 단수형에 –s를 붙여 복수형으로 만듭니다.

② –s, –x, –sh, –ch로 끝나는 명사는 뒤에 –es를 붙여 복수형으로 만듭니다.

③ –f, –fe로 끝나는 명사는 f나 fe를 v로 바꾸고 –es를 붙여 복수형으로 만듭니다.

④ 자음 + y로 끝나는 명사는 y를 i로 바꾸고 –es를 붙여 복수형으로 만듭니다.

Regular Plural Nouns			
+ -s	+ -es	f, fe ➡ v + -es	consonant + y ➡ i + -es
an apple ➡ apples	a bus ➡ buses	a lea**f** ➡ leaves	a pupp**y** ➡ puppies
a book ➡ books	a fox ➡ foxes	a wol**f** ➡ wolves	a bab**y** ➡ babies
a cat ➡ cats	a dish ➡ dishes	a scar**f** ➡ scarves	a cand**y** ➡ candies
a toy ➡ toys	a peach ➡ peaches	a kni**fe** ➡ knives	a butterf**ly** ➡ butterflies

A Read and write.

~~orange~~	knife	glass	cherry	book	brush
wife	country	scarf	baby	dish	toy

-s	-es	-ves	-ies
oranges			

 **Look and write.**

baby   leaf   ~~bus~~   scarf   cherry   bench

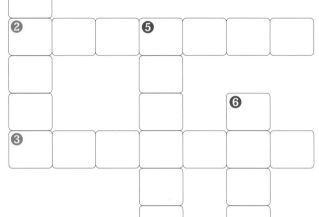

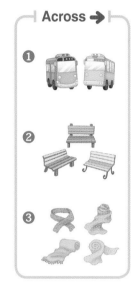
Across →

①
②
③

Down ↓

④
⑤
⑥

Write and match.

1 a watch → four __watches__

2 a tiger → three _____

3 a candy → seven _____

4 a wolf → two _____

D Look and write.

1

three __boys__ ➡ There are __three__ __boys__ .
      boy

2

two _____ ➡ There are _____ _____.
   strawberry

3

four _____ ➡ There are _____ _____.
   leaf

4

three _____ ➡ They have _____ _____.
   dish

5

six _____ ➡ He has _____ _____.
   key

E Look, read, and correct.

1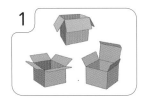

There are three boxs.
➡ __There are three boxes.__

2

There are three butterfly.
➡ _____

3

I have five knifees.
➡ _____

4

She has two rabbit.
➡ _____

Irregular Plural Nouns

GRAMMAR POINT

복수명사 (불규칙변화)

- 복수명사는 사람, 장소, 동물, 사물 등이 둘 이상임을 나타내며, 단수형에 –s나 –es를 붙여 복수형으로 만드는 규칙변화와 그렇지 않은 불규칙변화가 있습니다.
- 불규칙변화의 경우 단수와 복수의 형태가 같은 경우도 있고, 단수형과 전혀 다른 복수형을 취하기도 합니다.

Irregular Plural Nouns					
a man	➡ men	a goose	➡ geese	an ox	➡ oxen
a woman	➡ women	a sheep	➡ sheep	a child	➡ children
a foot	➡ feet	a deer	➡ deer	a person	➡ people
a tooth	➡ teeth	a fish	➡ fish	a mouse	➡ mice

A Read and write.

1 a tooth
➡ two ___teeth___

2 a fish
➡ four _____

3 a man
➡ ten _____

4 a child
➡ three _____

5 a mouse
➡ seven _____

6 a goose
➡ eight _____

7 an ox
➡ three _____

8 a woman
➡ five _____

9 a sheep
➡ ten _____

10 a deer
➡ six _____

11 a foot
➡ six _____

12 a person
➡ four _____

B Look, count, and write.

tooth	mouse	child	goose
foot	deer	~~fish~~	man	ox

1

____four____   ____fish____

2

_____   _____

3

_____   _____

4

_____   _____

5

_____   _____

6

_____   _____

7

_____   _____

8

_____   _____

9

_____   _____

C Read, circle, and write.

1 There is a _____woman_____ .
   (woman) / women)

2 There are seven _____.
   (fish / fishs)

3 There are twenty _____.
   (person / people)

4 The fox has a _____.
   (goose / geese)

5 My parents have four _____.
   (sheep / sheeps)

6 The farmer has three _____.
   (ox / oxen)

D Look and write.

1
an ____ox____ ➡ There is ____an____ ____ox____.
ox

2
six _____ ➡ There are _____ _____.
sheep

3
three _____ ➡ There are _____ _____.
woman

4
a _____ ➡ The cat has _____ _____.
fish

5
four _____ ➡ He has _____ _____.
goose

E Look, read, and correct.

1
There are three childs.
➡ _There are three children._____

2
There is a mice.
➡ _____

3
There are four person.
➡ _____

4
She has a geese.
➡ _____

5
They have three fishs.
➡ _____

Countable & Uncountable Nouns

GRAMMAR POINT

가산 명사 / 불가산 명사

- 명사에는 셀 수 있는 가산 명사와 셀 수 없는 불가산 명사가 있습니다.
- 가산 명사에는 단수형과 복수형이 있으며, 단수형 앞에는 하나를 의미하는 부정관사 a, an이나 숫자 one을 쓰고, 복수형 명사는 단수형을 복수형으로 만들고 앞에 갯수를 나타내는 숫자와 함께 쓰기도 합니다.
- 불가산 명사는 단수, 복수의 구별이 없으므로 복수형이 없습니다. 따라서 불가산 명사는 하나를 의미하는 부정관사나 갯수를 나타내는 숫자와 함께 쓸 수 없습니다.

Countable Nouns		Uncountable Nouns
Singular	**Plural**	
an elephant (코끼리 한 마리) a box (박스 한 개) one wolf (늑대 한 마리)	two elephants (코끼리 두 마리) five boxes (박스 다섯 개) two wolves (늑대 두 마리)	~~an~~ ice cream (아이스크림) ~~a~~ water (물) ~~one~~ cheese (치즈) ~~two~~ sugars (설탕)

A Write *C* for countable nouns and *UC* for uncountable nouns.

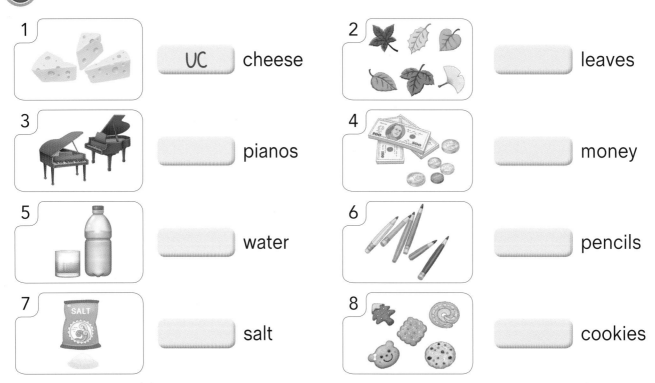

1. UC cheese
2. ___ leaves
3. ___ pianos
4. ___ money
5. ___ water
6. ___ pencils
7. ___ salt
8. ___ cookies

B Look and circle.

1

a I an I (X)
bread

2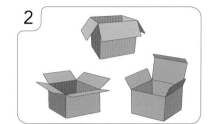

a I three I X
boxes

3

a I two I X
juice

4

a I an I X
umbrella

5

four I an I X
chocolate

6

a I four I X
fish

C Read and write.

milk	cookie	homework	juice
knife	bread	umbrella	puppy

Countable Nouns		Uncountable Nouns
Singular	**Plural**	
It is a cookie.	They are cookies.	It is milk.

D **Look and write.**

1

<u>Are</u> <u>they</u> peaches?

Yes, _____ _____.

2

_____ _____ ice cream?

Yes, _____ _____.

3

_____ _____ ___ book?

Yes, _____ _____.

4

_____ _____ ___ egg?

No, _____ _____.

It is _____ _____.

5

_____ _____ cheese?

No, _____ _____.

It is _____.

6

_____ _____ foxes?

No, _____ _____.

They are _____.

| butter | apple | wolf |

E **Read and correct.**

1 They are orange. → <u>They are oranges.</u>

2 It is an ice cream. → _____

3 It is a money. → _____

4 It is a umbrella. → _____

5 Is it cookie? → _____

6 Is it an orange juice? → _____

A/An/Some + Noun

GRAMMAR POINT

A / An / Some + 명사

- 셀 수 있는 단수명사 앞에는 '하나의'라는 의미를 가지는 부정관사 a나 an을 붙이며, 자음으로 시작하는 명사 앞에는 a를, 모음으로 시작하는 명사 앞에는 an을 씁니다.
- some은 '몇 개의' 또는 '약간의'라는 의미를 가지며, 셀 수 있는 명사의 복수형이나 셀 수 없는 명사 앞에 씁니다.
- some은 셀 수 있는 명사의 단수형 앞에는 쓸 수 없습니다.

a / an + singular noun	some + plural noun	some + uncountable noun	
an orange (오렌지 한 개)	some oranges (몇 개의 오렌지)	juice (주스)	➡ some juice (약간의 주스)
a watch (시계 한 개)	some watches (몇 개의 시계)	butter (버터)	➡ some butter (약간의 버터)
a knife (칼 한 개)	some knives (몇 개의 칼)	money (돈)	➡ some money (약간의 돈)
a candy (사탕 한 개)	some candies (몇 개의 사탕)	homework (숙제)	➡ some homework (약간의 숙제)

(A) **Read and write *a*, *an*, or *some*.**

1 _____an_____ egg

2 _____ crayon

3 _____ ice cream

4 _____ butterflies

5 _____ juice

6 _____ rabblt

7 _____ alligators

8 _____ milk

9 _____ homework

10 _____ octopus

B Read and write.

~~egg~~	leaf	~~chocolate~~	bread	water	goose
cookie	money	homework	salt	child	watch

┤ **some + countable noun** ├

some eggs _____

_____ _____

_____ _____

┤ **some + uncountable noun** ├

some chocolate _____

_____ _____

_____ _____

C Look and write *a*, *an*, or *some*.

1

There is _____an_____ igloo.

2

There are _____ flowers.

3

There is _____ butter.

4

There is _____ fox.

5

There is _____ umbrella.

6

There is _____ bread.

D Look and write.

1

The mice have ___an___ ___orange___ .

They have __some__ __cookies__ .

2

Tom has _____ _____ .

He has _____ _____ .

3

Amy and I have _____ _____ .

We have _____ _____ .

4

The horse has _____ _____ .

It has _____ _____ .

| ~~orange~~ | candy | water | cheese |
| carrot | bread | ~~cookie~~ | money |

E Read and correct.

1 There is a milk. → __There is some milk.__

2 There is some umbrella. → _____

3 There is a orange. → _____

4 She has some book. → _____

5 We have some moneys. → _____

6 They have some juices. → _____

Units 1-4

A Look, count, and write.

| butterfly | watch | toy | leaf | ~~peach~~ | igloo |

1 a peach   two peaches

2 _____   _____

3 _____   _____

4 _____   _____

5 _____   _____

6 _____   _____

B Read and write.

Singular	Plural	Singular	Plural	Singular	Plural
goose	geese	mouse			people
	men		deer	woman	
sheep			oxen		children
	teeth	foot			fish

C **Read, circle, and write.**

1   It is _____milk_____.

   a apple   (b) milk   c mice

2   They are _____.

   a cheese   b a wolf   c geese

3   It is _____.

   a moneys   b an orange   c watch

4   Are they _____? Yes, they _____.

   a peaches, are   b an igloo, are   c bread, is

5   Is it an _____? No, it isn't. It is _____.

   a hat, candies   b ice cream, a cheese   c ostrich, a goose

D **Read and write.**

| onion | women | teacher | ant | igloo | piano |
| wolves | orange | homework | bread | bench | chair |

a	an	some
_____	_____onion_____	_____
_____	_____	_____
_____	_____	_____
_____	_____	_____

Possessive Adjectives

GRAMMAR POINT

소유격

- 소유격은 명사 앞에 쓰여, 명사가 누구에게 속한 것인지를 나타냅니다.
- 인칭대명사 I, You, He, She, It, We, They의 소유격은 각각 my, your, his, her, its, our, their이며 '~의'로 해석합니다.
- 명사의 소유격은 명사 뒤에 's를 붙여 만듭니다.
- Whose는 소유에 대해 물어보는 의문사로 뒤에 명사가 와서 '~은 누구의 것입니까?'라고 해석합니다.

Subject Pronouns		Possessive Adjectives	
I	my	This is my toy. (이것은 나의 장난감이다.)	/ My toy is red. (나의 장난감은 빨간색이다.)
you	your	This is your toy. (이것은 너의 장난감이다.)	/ Your toy is red. (너의 장난감은 빨간색이다.)
he	his	This is his toy. (이것은 그의 장난감이다.)	/ His toy is red. (그의 장난감은 빨간색이다.)
she	her	This is her toy. (이것은 그녀의 장난감이다.)	/ Her toy is red. (그녀의 장난감은 빨간색이다.)
it	its	This is its toy. (이것은 그것의 장난감이다.)	/ Its toy is red. (그것의 장난감은 빨간색이다.)
we	our	This is our toy. (이것은 우리의 장난감이다.)	/ Our toy is red. (우리의 장난감은 빨간색이다.)
they	their	This is their toy. (이것은 그들의 장난감이다.)	/ Their toy is red. (그들의 장난감은 빨간색이다.)
Amy	Amy's	This is Amy's toy. (이것은 에이미의 장난감이다.)	/ Amy's toy is red. (에이미의 장난감은 빨간색이다.)

A Read and write.

1 I + computer
→ _my computer_

2 you + pencil
→ _____

3 she + teddy bear
→ _____

4 he + glove
→ _____

5 Lisa + glasses
→ _____

6 it + bone
→ _____

7 we + house
→ _____

8 you + socks
→ _____

9 they + cat
→ _____

B **Read, circle, and write.**

1 _____She_____ is my teacher.
   (She / Her)

2 That is _____ cat Cleo.
              (I / my)

3 This is _____ umbrella.
               (you / your)

4 _____ house is big.
      (We / Our)

5 These are _____ shoes.
                  (he / his)

C **Look and write.**

1
This is _____my_____ piano.

2
That is _____ watch.

3
These are _____ pencils.

4
Those are _____ rain boots.

5
_____ shoes are yellow.

6
_____ fish is big.

D Read, write, and find the correct question.

1 [D] They are _____my_____ socks.
   <small>I</small>

2 [ ] It is _____ doll.
   <small>she</small>

3 [ ] They are _____ robots.
   <small>we</small>

4 [ ] It is _____ eraser.
   <small>Jane</small>

5 [ ] They are _____ pants.
   <small>he</small>

6 [ ] It is _____ glass shoe.
   <small>Cinderella</small>

7 [ ] They are _____ pencils.
   <small>you</small>

8 [ ] It is _____ bone.
   <small>the dog</small>

A Whose pants are they?   **B** Whose doll is it?

C Whose glass shoe is it?   **D** Whose socks are they?

E Whose robots are they?   **F** Whose eraser is it?

G Whose bone is it?   **H** Whose pencils are they?

E Read and correct.

1 This is you umbrella. ➔ This is your umbrella.

2 She jacket is pink. ➔ _____

3 They necks are long. ➔ _____

4 That is you book. ➔ _____

5 Who glove is it? ➔ _____

6 Those are they boots. ➔ _____

UNIT 06 Possessive Pronouns

GRAMMAR POINT

소유대명사

● 소유대명사는 소유를 나타내는 대명사로 〈소유격 + 명사〉 대신 쓰이며, '~의 것'이라는 의미를 갖습니다.

● 인칭대명사의 소유격에는 my, your, his, her, our, their, its가 있으며, 이것들의 소유대명사는 각각 mine, yours, his, hers, ours, theirs입니다. 다만 its는 소유대명사를 사용하지 않으며, 명사의 소유대명사는 명사 뒤에 's를 붙여서 만듭니다.

Possessive Adjectives		Possessive Pronouns	
my	mine	This is my pen. (이것은 나의 펜이다.)	= This pen is mine. (이 펜은 나의 것이다.)
your	yours	This is your pen. (이것은 너의 펜이다.)	= This pen is yours. (이 펜은 너의 것이다.)
his	his	This is his pen. (이것은 그의 펜이다.)	= This pen is his. (이 펜은 그의 것이다.)
her	hers	This is her pen. (이것은 그녀의 펜이다.)	= This pen is hers. (이 펜은 그녀의 것이다.)
our	ours	This is our pen. (이것은 우리의 펜이다.)	= This pen is ours. (이 펜은 우리의 것이다.)
their	theirs	This is their pen. (이것은 그들의 펜이다.)	= This pen is theirs. (이 펜은 그들의 것이다.)
Amy's	Amy's	This is Amy's pen. (이것은 에이미의 펜이다.)	= This pen is Amy's. (이 펜은 에이미의 것이다.)

A Look and write.

1
This is my camera.
= This is ___mine___.

2
These are our bikes.
= These are _____.

3
This is her house.
= This is _____.

4
Those are their candies.
= Those are _____.

5
That is his car.
= That is _____.

6
These are your balloons.
= These are _____.

B Read and change.

1 That is your bicycle.   = That bicycle is _____yours_____ .

2 This is my backpack.   = This backpack is _____ .

3 These are his glasses.   = These glasses are _____ .

4 Those are her crayons.   = Those crayons are _____ .

5 That is their camera.   = That camera is _____ .

6 These are our mittens.   = These mittens are _____ .

7 This is Amy's pencil case. = This pencil case is _____ .

C Look and write.

In My Backpack

In Her Backpack

In His Backpack

1 Whose watch is it? It is ___her___ watch (= _hers_).

2 Whose scarf is it? It is _____ scarf (= _____).

3 Whose chocolate is it? It is _____ chocolate (= _____).

4 Whose toys are they? They are _____ toys (= _____).

5 Whose books are they? They are _____ books (= _____).

6 Whose pencils are they? They are _____ pencils (= _____).

D Look, read, and change.

1

That is his glove.

→ <u>That glove is his.</u>

2

This is my phone.

→ _____

3

These are your skates.

→ _____

4
Those are their candies.

→ _____

5

These are her knives.

→ _____

6

That is our house.

→ _____

E Read and correct.

1 These crayons are her. → <u>These crayons are hers.</u>

2 This skateboard is he. → _____

3 That computer is my. → _____

4 These oranges are your. → _____

5 Who umbrella is it? → _____

6 Who glasses are they? → _____

UNIT 07 Object Pronouns (Singular)

GRAMMAR POINT

목적격 대명사 (단수)

- 대명사는 명사를 대신하여 사용하는 말로, 대명사가 문장에서 주어로 사용되면 주격 대명사라고 하고, 목적어로 사용되면 목적격 대명사라고 합니다.
- 한 사람 또는 한 개를 의미하는 단수 인칭대명사 주격에는 I, you, he, she, it가 있으며, 이것들의 목적격 대명사는 각각 me, you, him, her, it입니다.
- 단수 인칭대명사의 목적격 대명사는 '~을' 또는 '~를'이라고 해석합니다.

Subject Pronouns	Object Pronouns (Singular)	
I	me	Tom likes me. (탐은 나를 좋아합니다.)
you	you	Tom likes you. (탐은 당신을 좋아합니다.)
he	him	Tom likes him. (탐은 그를 좋아합니다.)
she	her	Tom likes her. (탐은 그녀를 좋아합니다.)
it	it	Tom likes it. (탐은 그것을 좋아합니다.)

A Look, circle, and write.

1. My parents know __you__ . (you / your)

2.  The puppies likes _____ . (I / me)

3. The girl has _____ . (it's / it)

4. The cats like _____ . (her / she)

5. The students like _____ . (he / him)

6.  They want _____ . (it / it's)

B **Read and write.**

	Subject Pronouns	Object Pronouns	Sentences
1	I	_____me_____	My grandparents love _____me_____.
2	you	_____	The cat likes _____.
3	he	_____	Sally doesn't know _____.
4	she	_____	The police officer helps _____.
5	it	_____	The boys don't have _____.

C **Look and write.**

1

The boy helps _____her_____.

2

My grandparents like _____.

3

Your parents love _____.

4

The girl eats _____.

5

Does Lisa like her sister?
No, she doesn't like _____.

6

Do they want the bike?
Yes, they want _____.

D Read and unscramble.

1 [I] [her.] [like]

➡ _I like her._

2 [knows] [My sister] [him.]

➡ _____

3 [likes] [The puppy] [you.]

➡ _____

4 [doesn't] [She] [me.] [like]

➡ _____

5 [him.] [friends] [like] [His]

➡ _____

6 [We] [have] [it.] [don't]

➡ _____

E Read and correct.

1 The student has it's.   ➡ _The student has it._

2 My brother likes she.   ➡ _____

3 The cat doesn't like he.   ➡ _____

4 Jane rides it's every day. ➡ _____

5 The boy likes I.   ➡ _____

6 Your parents love your.   ➡ _____

Object Pronouns (Plural)

GRAMMAR PoINT

목적격 대명사 (복수)

- 대명사는 명사를 대신하여 사용하는 말로, 대명사가 문장에서 목적어로 사용되면 목적격 대명사라고 합니다.
- 두 사람 혹은 두 개 이상을 의미하는 복수 인칭대명사 주격에는 we, you, they가 있으며, 이것들의 목적격 대명사는 각각 us, you, them입니다.
- 복수 인칭대명사의 목적격 대명사는 '～들을' 또는 '～를'이라고 해석합니다.

Subject Pronouns	Object Pronouns (Plural)	
we you they	us you them	Tom likes us. (탐은 우리를 좋아합니다.) Tom likes you. (탐은 당신들을 좋아합니다.) Tom likes them. (탐은 그들을 좋아합니다.)

A Read, check, and write.

1 The dog likes ___them___ .   ☐ they   ✓ them   ☐ their

2 Our grandparents love _____ .   ☐ we   ☐ our   ☐ us

3 They know _____ .   ☐ you   ☐ your   ☐ you're

4 Amy doesn't eat _____ .   ☐ they   ☐ them   ☐ their

5 Mr. Brown teaches _____ .   ☐ us   ☐ we   ☐ our

6 Your friends help _____ .   ☐ your   ☐ you   ☐ you're

7 We don't like _____ .   ☐ they   ☐ their   ☐ them

B Read, write, and match.

1 The puppies like <u>you and Tom</u>.

→ They like <u>   you   </u>.

2 The girl doesn't like <u>the iguanas</u>.

→ She doesn't like <u>   </u>.

3 Your father loves <u>you and your brother</u>.

→ He loves <u>   </u>.

4 Our mother loves <u>my sister and me</u>.

→ She loves <u>   </u>.

5 Amy eats <u>the sandwiches</u>.

→ She eats <u>   </u>.

C Read and change.

1 They have <u>flowers</u>. → They have <u> them </u>.

2 Come and see <u>Dad, Mom, and me</u>. → Come and see <u>   </u>.

3 We like <u>you and your sister</u>. → We like <u>   </u>.

4 Thank you for <u>the shoes</u>. → Thank you for <u>   </u>.

5 He teaches <u>my friend and me</u>. → He teaches <u>   </u>.

6 The cats don't like <u>you and Lisa</u>. → The cats don't like <u>   </u>.

D Read and unscramble.

1 [The boy] [them.] [wants]

→ The boy wants them.

2 [know] [us.] [Your parents]

→ _____

3 [helps] [you.] [Mrs. Brown]

→ _____

4 [don't] [They] [you.] [like]

→ _____

5 [like] [The cat] [us.] [doesn't]

→ _____

6 [The students] [don't] [them.] [have]

→ _____

E Read and correct.

1 I like your very much. → I like you very much.

2 Our teacher loves we. → _____

3 The twins don't know your. → _____

4 The boy doesn't want their. → _____

5 I don't have they. → _____

6 They don't like our. → _____

A Read and write.

	Subject Pronouns	Possessive Adjectives	Sentences
1	I	___my___	___My___ cat is cute.
2	you	_____	This is _____ ice cream.
3	he	_____	These are _____ robots.
4	she	_____	_____ dress is pretty.
5	it	_____	_____ tail is long.
6	they	_____	That is _____ house.
7	we	_____	Whose car is it? It is _____ car.

B Write the possessive pronouns.

1
This umbrella is ___hers___.

2
That house is _____.

3
These balls are _____.

4
Whose camera is it?
It is _____.

5
Whose bananas are they?
They are _____.

6
Whose pencil case is it?
It is _____.

C **Read, choose, and write.**

1
| she |
| her | she's |

We don't know _____her_____ .

2
| they |
| them | their |

The penguins have _____ .

3
| he's |
| he | him |

Lisa doesn't like _____ .

4
| you |
| your | you're |

Your parents love _____ .

5
| I |
| me | my |

My father helps _____ .

D **Read, circle, and write.**

1 _____His_____ bicycle is new.

　ⓐ Him　　　　　　ⓑ His　　　　　　ⓒ He

2 These are _____ cats.

　ⓐ our　　　　　　ⓑ we　　　　　　ⓒ you

3 Those books are _____ .

　ⓐ mine　　　　　　ⓑ I　　　　　　ⓒ my

4 _____ shoes are they? They are _____ .

　ⓐ Whose, her　　　ⓑ Who, hers　　　ⓒ Whose, hers

5 Do you like the bike? Yes, I like _____ very much.

　ⓐ it　　　　　　ⓑ them　　　　　　ⓒ it's

Present Simple (Affirmatives)

GRAMMAR POINT

현재시제 (긍정문)

- 현재시제는 현재의 사실, 반복적인 습관이나 행동을 말할 때 사용합니다.
- 현재시제 긍정문에서 주어가 I, You, We, They 또는 복수명사일 때 동사는 원형을 쓰고, He, She, It 또는 단수명사일 때는 3인칭 현재시제 동사를 사용합니다. 3인칭 현재동사는 다음과 같이 만들 수 있습니다.
  ① 규칙 동사
    - 대부분의 동사 뒤에 −s를 붙입니다.
    - −s, −x, −sh, −ch로 끝나는 동사는 뒤에 −es 붙입니다.
    - 자음 + y로 끝나는 동사는 y를 i로 바꾸고 −es를 붙입니다.
  ② 불규칙 동사: 특별한 규칙이 없습니다.

Present Simple (Affirmatives)			
I (나는) You (당신은 / 당신들은) We (우리는) They (그들은)	drink milk. (우유를 마십니다.)	He (그는) She (그녀는) It (그것은) Jane (제인은)	drinks milk. (우유를 마십니다.)

Regular Verbs (규칙 동사)		Irregular Verbs (불규칙 동사)	
+ -s	drink ➡ drinks (마시다), play ➡ plays (연주하다)	have ➡ has (가지고 있다)	
+ -es	watch ➡ watches (보다), brush ➡ brushes (양치질하다)	go ➡ goes (가다)	
y ➡ i + -es	study ➡ studies (공부하다), cry ➡ cries (울다)	do ➡ does (하다)	

A Read and write.

	I / You / We / They	He / She / It		I / You / We / They	He / She / It
mix	mix	mixes	teach		
have			cry		
write			do		
ride			study		

B Read, circle, and write.

1 He __brushes__ his teeth.
(brush / brushes)

2 They _____ kites.
(flies / fly)

3 I _____ spaghetti.
(cook / cooks)

4 The baby _____.
(cries / cry)

5 She _____ her face.
(wash / washes)

6 We _____ a walk.
(take / takes)

7 You _____ a horse.
(rides / ride)

8 Mr. Jones _____ TV.
(watch / watches)

C Look and write.

1
teach

He __teaches__ English.

2
fly

Tom _____ a kite.

3
go

They _____ to the park.

4
study

I _____ math every day.

5
write

She _____ an email.

6
have

The cook _____ a dish.

D Read and change.

1 They <u>watch TV</u>. → He _____watches TV_____.

2 The babies <u>cry</u>. → The cat _____.

3 You <u>read comic books</u>. → He _____.

4 I <u>go to school</u>. → She _____.

5 The monkeys <u>have bananas</u>. → It _____.

6 We <u>study English</u>. → Sally _____.

7 I <u>ride a bike</u>. → Tom _____.

8 My parents <u>cook dinner</u>. → My mother _____.

9 You <u>fly a kite</u>. → The boy _____.

E Read and correct.

1 She wash her face. → She washes her face.

2 The cats cries at night. → _____

3 Tom do his homework. → _____

4 You brushes your teeth. → _____

5 I writes an email. → _____

6 He play the flute. → _____

Present Simple (Negatives)

GRAMMAR POINT

현재시제 (부정문)

- 현재시제는 현재의 사실, 반복적인 습관이나 행동을 말할 때 사용합니다.
- 현재시제에서 주어가 I, You, We, They 또는 복수명사일 때 부정문을 만드는 방법은 주어 다음에 don't (= do not)를 쓰고 다음에 동사원형을 씁니다.
- 현재시제에서 주어가 He, She, It 또는 단수명사일 때 부정문을 만드는 방법은 주어 다음에 doesn't (= does not)를 쓰고 다음에 동사원형을 씁니다.
- 현재시제의 부정문은 '～하지 않는다'라고 해석합니다.

Present Simple (Negatives)					
I (나는) You (당신은 / 당신들은) We (우리는) They (그들은)	don't (～ 하지 않는다)	drink (마시다) wash (씻다) study (공부하다) have (가지고 있다) go (가다)	He (그는) She (그녀는) It (그것은)	doesn't (～ 하지 않는다)	drink (마시다) wash (씻다) study (공부하다) have (가지고 있다) go (가다)

*don't = do not / doesn't = does not

A **Read and write** *don't* **or** *doesn't*.

1 I play.
  → I ___don't___ play.

2 He eats.
  → He _____ eat.

3 You cry
  → You _____ cry.

4 She watches.
  → She _____ watch.

5 It runs.
  → It _____ run.

6 We study.
  → We _____ study.

7 They go.
  → They _____ go.

8 It flies.
  → It _____ fly.

1
play

She __plays__ the piano.

She __doesn't__ __play__ the flute.

2
drink

He _____ milk.

He _____ _____ coffee.

3
go

You _____ to an art class.

You _____ _____ to the park.

4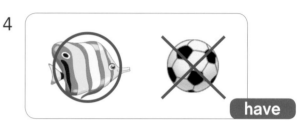
have

It _____ a fish.

It _____ _____ a soccer ball.

5
wash

They _____ their faces.

They _____ _____ their feet.

6
study

I _____ Chinese.

I _____ _____ English.

C Read and write.

1 He / not / fly a kite → __He doesn't fly a kite.__

2 She / not / ride a bike → _____

3 My parents / not / watch TV → _____

4 The cat / not / sleep → _____

5 You / not / play tennis → _____

D Read and unscramble.

1 [study] [They] [don't] [French.]

→ _They don't study French._

2 [doesn't] [a car.] [He] [drive]

→ _____

3 [My parents] [coffee.] [don't] [drink]

→ _____

4 [He] [clean] [his room.] [doesn't]

→ _____

5 [at night.] [doesn't] [bark] [The dog]

→ _____

6 [play] [We] [basketball.] [don't]

→ _____

E Read and correct.

1 I doesn't read comic books. → _I don't read comic books._

2 You don't listens to music. → _____

3 We doesn't play soccer. → _____

4 Lisa don't have a brother. → _____

5 We don't goes to the park. → _____

6 The giraffe don't eat carrots. → _____

Present Simple (Yes / No Questions)

GRAMMAR POINT

현재시제 (의문문)

- 주어가 I, You, We, They 또는 복수명사 일 때 현재시제 의문문은 문장의 맨 앞에 Do를 붙여
  Do + 주어 + 동사원형 ...?의 형태를 사용합니다.
- 주어가 He, She, It 또는 단수명사일 때 현재시제 의문문은 문장의 맨 앞에 Does를 붙여
  Does + 주어 + 동사원형 ...?의 형태를 사용합니다.
- Do나 Does로 시작하는 의문문은 Yes나 No로 대답하며, 긍정일 때는 Yes, 주어 + do / does.로, 부정일 때는
  No, 주어 + don't / doesn't.로 대답합니다.

Question	Answer	
Do I / you / we / you / they sleep? (나는 / 당신은 / 우리는 / 당신들은 / 그들은 잠을 잡니까?)	Yes, you / I / you / we / they do. (네, 그렇습니다.)	No, you / I / you / we / they don't. (아니오, 그렇지 않습니다.)
Does he / she / it sleep? (그는 / 그녀는 / 그것은 잠을 잡니까?)	Yes, he / she / it does. (네, 그렇습니다.)	No, he / she / it doesn't. (아니오, 그렇지 않습니다.)

A Read and write.

1 ___Do___ you study English?
Yes, I ___do___.

2 _____ he drink juice?
No, he _____.

3 _____ she eat breakfast?
Yes, she _____.

4 _____ they play soccer?
No, they _____.

5 _____ it climb a tree?
No, it _____.

6 _____ we listen to music?
Yes, you _____.

B **Read and write.**

1 teach   _Does_ he _teach_ English?

2 sleep   _____ it _____ at night?

3 play   _____ the children _____ soccer?

4 cry   _____ they _____ at night?

5 read   _____ she _____ comic books?

6 go   _____ Ben and Ken _____ to school?

7 watch   _____ your sister _____ TV?

C **Look and write.**

_____Do_____ you _____teach_____ math?

_____Yes_____, _____I_____ _____do_____.

_____ she _____ dinner?

_____, _____ _____.

_____ they _____ bikes?

_____, _____ _____.

_____ he _____ a car?

_____, _____ _____.

drive

cook

ride

~~teach~~

D Read and unscramble.

1 play | you | the violin? | Do

→ Do you play the violin?

2 she | Does | English? | study

→ _____

3 TV? | Do | watch | they

→ _____

4 Does | a tree? | clime | the monkey

→ _____

5 fly | he | a kite? | Does

→ _____

6 your parents | Do | breakfast? | eat

→ _____

E Read and correct.

1 Does they go to the park?   → Do they go to the park?

2 Do you reads storybooks?   → _____

3 Does he drives a car?   → _____

4 Does Tom washes his feet?   → _____

5 Do the owl sleep at night?   → _____

6 Does your parents watch TV? → _____

Simple Present (What Questions)

GRAMMAR POINT

현재시제 (What 의문문)

- What은 의문사로 의문문의 맨 앞에 위치하며, '무엇을'이라고 해석합니다.
- 주어가 I, You, We, They 또는 복수명사일 때, What으로 시작하는 현재시제 의문문은 What + do + 주어 + 동사원형 ...?의 형태를 사용합니다.
- 주어가 He, She, It 또는 단수명사일 때, What으로 시작하는 현재시제 의문문은 What + does + 주어 + 동사원형 ...?의 형태를 사용합니다.
- 의문사 What으로 시작하는 의문문은 Yes나 No로 대답하지 않습니다.

Question			Answer		
What do	I you we you they	do?	You I You We They	drink	milk.
(나는 / 당신은 / 우리는 / 당신들을 / 그들은 무엇을 합니까?)			(당신은 / 나는 / 당신들은 / 우리는 / 그들은 우유를 마십니다.)		
What does	he she it	do?	He She It	drinks	milk.
(그는 / 그녀는 / 그것은 무엇을 합니까?)			(그는 / 그녀는 / 그것은 우유를 마십니다.)		

A Read, write, and check.

1 What ___do___ you do?   ✓ I read a book.   ☐ Yes, I do.

2 What _____ we do?   ☐ No, you don't.   ☐ You eat bananas.

3 What _____ he do?   ☐ Yes, he does.   ☐ He studies math.

4 What _____ they do?   ☐ They ride bikes.   ☐ No, they don't.

5 What _____ she do?   ☐ Yes, she does.   ☐ She plays the cello.

B Look and write.

1

    __What__ __do__ they do?

    They brush their teeth.

2

    _____ _____ she do?

    She eats breakfast.

3

    _____ _____ you do?

    We watch TV.

4

    _____ _____ he do?

    He reads a newspaper.

C Look and write.

1 __What__ __does__ he do every day?

  __He__ __rides__ a bike.

ride

2 _____ _____ they do after school?

  _____ _____ kites.

fly

3 _____ _____ she do in the evening?

  _____ _____ dinner.

cook

4 _____ _____ the cat do at night?

  _____ _____ a mouse.

chase

D Read and unscramble.

1 | she | What | do? | does |

→ What does she do?

2 | do | they | What | do? |

→ _____

3 | do? | does | Harry | What |

→ _____

4 | What | do? | does | the dog |

→ _____

5 | your parents | do? | do | What |

→ _____

E Read and correct.

1 Q What does you do?　→ What do you do?

A I does my homework.　→ _____

2 Q What does he does?　→ _____

A He drink orange juice.　→ _____

3 Q What do your mother do?　→ _____

A She brush her teeth.　→ _____

A Read and write.

1

go

• I ____go____ to the park.

• He ____goes____ to the swimming pool.

2

drink

• We _____ orange juice.

• Kate _____ hot chocolate.

3

fly

• You _____ a model airplane.

• My friend _____ a kite.

4

catch

• They _____ some fish.

• The cat _____ a mouse.

B Look and write.

1

eat

She ___eats___ spaghetti.

She ___doesn't___ ___eat___ salad.

2

teach

He _____ English.

He _____ _____ math.

3

have

We _____ umbrellas.

We _____ _____ rain boots.

4

watch

They _____ TV.

They _____ _____ a DVD.

C Look and write.

1

_____Do_____ they cry at night?

Yes, ___they___ ___do___.

2

_____ he go to the park?

No, _____ _____.

3

_____ you teach math?

Yes, _____ _____.

4

_____ she cook dinner?

No, _____ _____.

D Read, circle, and write.

1 _____What_____ do you do? I watch TV.

   a Who   (b) What   c Whose

2 What _____ she do? She plays the piano.

   a is   b do   c does

3 What do they do? _____ English.

   a They study   b Yes, they study c It studies

4 What does he _____? He _____ juice.

   a do, drink   b do, drinks   c does, drinks

5 What _____ your mother _____? She reads books.

   a does, do   b does, does   c do, does

Present Continuous (Affirmatives)

GRAMMAR POINT

현재진행시제 (긍정문)

- 현재진행시제는 현재 진행중인 동작을 나타내며, '~하고 있는 중이다'라고 해석합니다.
- 현재진행시제는 be 동사의 현재형 + 〈동사원형 -ing〉의 형태를 취하며, 〈동사원형 -ing〉를 만드는 방법은 다음과 같습니다.
  ① 대부분의 동사는 동사원형에 -ing를 붙입니다.
  ② -e로 끝나는 동사는 e를 지우고 -ing를 붙입니다.
  ③ 단모음 + 단자음으로 끝나는 동사는 마지막 자음을 한 번 더 쓰고 -ing를 붙입니다.

Present Continuous (Affirmatives)		
I	am	sleeping. (나는 잠을 자고 있습니다.)
You	are	sleeping. (당신은 잠을 자고 있습니다.)
He / She / It	is	sleeping. (그는 / 그녀는 / 그것은 잠을 자고 있습니다.)
We / You / They	are	sleeping. (우리는 / 당신들은 / 그들은 잠을 자고 있습니다.)

+ -ing	-e + -ing	double consonant + -ing
play ➡ playing	make ➡ making	run ➡ running
sing ➡ singing	dance ➡ dancing	swim ➡ swimming
walk ➡ walking	drive ➡ driving	hit ➡ hitting

A Read and write.

1 run ⇒ running

2 sit ⇒ _____

3 cook ⇒ _____

4 climb ⇒ _____

5 ride ⇒ _____

6 drive ⇒ _____

7 sleep ⇒ _____

8 hit ⇒ _____

9 dance ⇒ _____

10 swim ⇒ _____

B **Read and write *am*, *is*, or *are*.**

1 She ___is___ cooking.

2 I _____ watching.

3 You _____ running.

4 He _____ making.

5 We _____ riding.

6 It _____ sitting.

7 They _____ swimming.

8 The bird _____ singing.

9 My parents _____ working.

10 Lisa _____ writing.

C **Look and write.**

1
brush

He ___is___ ___brushing___ his teeth.

2
write

She _____ _____ an email.

3
swim

The penguin _____ _____.

4
dance

You _____ _____.

5
go

The students _____ _____ to school.

6
cut

I _____ _____ some paper.

D **Look and write.**

teach	drive	walk	sit	eat

1. The birds <u>are</u> <u>sitting</u>.

2. My father _____ _____ a car.

3. They _____ _____.

4. I _____ _____ English.

5. Snow White _____ _____ an apple.

E **Read and correct.**

1. He are swimming. ➡ <u>He is swimming.</u>

2. They are danceing. ➡ _____

3. We building a sandcastle. ➡ _____

4. I cutting am some paper. ➡ _____

5. He is fly a kite. ➡ _____

6. You is watching TV. ➡ _____

UNIT 14 Present Continuous (Negatives)

GRAMMAR POINT

현재진행시제 (부정문)

- 현재진행시제의 부정문은 be 동사의 현재형 + not + 〈동사원형 –ing〉의 형태를 사용하며, '~하고 있지 않다'라고 해석합니다.
- 현재진행시제의 부정문에서도 be 동사 + not을 줄여서 is not → isn't, are not → aren't로 쓰고, I am not은 줄여서 I'm not으로 씁니다.

Present Continuous (Negatives)		
I	am not (= 'm not)	swimming. (나는 수영을 하고 있지 않습니다.)
You	are not (= aren't)	swimming. (당신은 수영을 하고 있지 않습니다.)
He / She / It	is not (= isn't)	swimming. (그는 / 그녀는 / 그것은 수영을 하고 있지 않습니다.)
We / You / They	are not (= aren't)	swimming. (우리는 / 당신들은 / 그들은 수영을 하고 있지 않습니다.)

A Read and write.

1 She is sleeping.
→ She ___isn't___ sleeping.

2 I am climbing.
→ I _____ climbing.

3 They are writing.
→ They _____ writing.

4 He is swimming.
→ He _____ swimming.

5 You are running.
→ You _____ running.

6 My mother is cooking.
→ My mother _____ cooking.

7 The dogs are barking.
→ The dogs _____ barking.

8 We are dancing.
→ We _____ dancing.

9 The mouse is chasing.
→ The mouse _____ chasing.

10 It is eating.
→ It _____ eating.

B Look and write.

1 You <u>aren't</u> <u>singing</u> a song.
You are dancing.

2 The cat _____ _____ a mouse.
It is sleeping.

3 We _____ _____ some paper.
We are swimming.

4 I _____ _____ _____ an email.
I am walking.

5 They _____ _____ baseball.
They are running.

write
~~sing~~
chase
play
cut

C Read and write.

1 I / not / swim → <u>I'm not swimming.</u>

2 They / not / ride → _____

3 Lisa / not / write → _____

4 The dog / not / bark → _____

5 You / not / hit → _____

6 We / not / study → _____

50

D Unscramble and write.

1
| isn't | He |
| doing |
| his homework. |

→ He isn't doing his homework.

2
| You | hitting |
| aren't |
| a ball. |

→ _____

3
| My mom |
| dinner. | isn't |
| cooking |

→ _____

4
| playing |
| soccer. | aren't |
| They |

→ _____

5
| I'm | driving |
| not |
| a car. |

→ _____

E Read and correct.

1 She isn't watch TV.   → She isn't watching TV.

2 They isn't dancing.   → _____

3 We aren't swiming.   → _____

4 The owl not is sleeping.   → _____

5 You drinking aren't milk.   → _____

6 I'm riding not a bike.   → _____

Present Continuous (Yes / No Questions)

GRAMMAR POINT

현재진행시제 (의문문)

- 현재진행시제 의문문은 be 동사의 현재형 + 주어 + 〈동사원형 −ing〉 ...?의 형태를 사용하며, '∼하고 있니?'라고 해석합니다.
- 현재진행시제의 의문문에 대한 대답은 Yes나 No로 하며, 긍정일 때는 Yes, 주어 + be 동사.를 부정일 때는 No, 주어 + be 동사 + not.을 사용하며, 부정일 경우에는 be 동사 + not을 줄인 축약형을 사용할 수 있습니다.

Question	Answer
Am I running? (나는 달리고 있습니까?)	Yes, you are. / No, you aren't.
Are you running? (당신은 달리고 있습니까?)	Yes, I am. / No, I'm not.
Is he running? (그는 달리고 있습니까?)	Yes, he is. / No, he isn't.
Is she running? (그녀는 달리고 있습니까?)	Yes, she is. / No, she isn't.
Is it running? (그것은 달리고 있습니까?)	Yes, it is. / No, it isn't.
Are we running? (우리는 달리고 있습니까?)	Yes, you are. / No, you aren't.
Are you running? (당신들은 달리고 있습니까?)	Yes, we are. / No, we aren't.
Are they running? (그들은 달리고 있습니까?)	Yes, they are. / No, they aren't.
	(네, 그렇습니다.) / (아니요, 그렇지 않습니다.)

A Read and write.

1 cut ___Is___ she ___cutting___ some paper?

2 drink _____ we _____ milk?

3 sing _____ they _____ a song?

4 run _____ your mother _____?

5 write _____ he _____ an email?

6 ride _____ you _____ a bike?

B **Look and write the answer.**

1

Is he catching a ball?

➡ _____No, he isn't._____

2

Are they cutting some paper?

➡ _____

3

Is she driving a car?

➡ _____

4

Are you reading a book?

➡ _____

5

Is the penguin swimming?

➡ _____

6

Are we riding horses?

➡ _____

C **Read and write.**

1 | she / eat / an apple | ➡ _____Is she eating an apple?_____

2 | you / hit / a ball | ➡ _____

3 | Tom / write / a letter | ➡ _____

4 | I / do / my homework | ➡ _____

5 | they / study / English | ➡ _____

6 | it / climb / a tree | ➡ _____

D Look and write.

1

swim

Are the ducklings ___swimming___?
Yes, ___they___ ___are___.

2

drive

_____ your mother _____ a car?
No, _____ _____.

3

dance

_____ you _____?
_____, _____ _____.

4

walk

_____ the penguins _____?
_____, _____ _____.

5

eat

_____ Snow White _____ an apple?
_____, _____ _____.

6
run

_____ the children _____?
_____, _____ _____.

E Read and correct.

1 Are he driving a car? → Is he driving a car?

2 Are she brushing her hair? → _____

3 Is he paint a picture? → _____

4 Are the parrot talking? Yes, it is. → _____

5 Are they fly? No, they aren't. → _____

6 Are you running? Yes, I is. → _____

UNIT 16 Present Continuous (Wh- Questions)

GRAMMAR POINT

현재진행시제 (의문사가 있는 의문문)

● What이나 Who는 의문사로 의문문의 맨 앞에 오며, 문장에서 각각 목적어와 주어의 역할을 합니다.

● 현재진행시제에서 What이 들어가는 의문문은 What + be 동사 + 주어 + doing?의 어순이며, What이 목적어 역할을 하여 '무엇을'이라고 해석합니다.

● 현재진행시제에서 Who가 들어가는 의문문은 Who + be 동사 + 〈동사원형 –ing〉?의 어순이며, Who가 주어 역할을 하여 '누가'라고 해석합니다.

● 의문사 What이나 Who로 시작하는 의문문은 Yes나 No로 대답하지 않습니다.

What Question				Answer		
What	am	I		You	are	
What	are	you	doing?	I	am	drinking.
What	is	he / she / it		He / She / It	is	
What	are	we / you / they		You / We / They	are	
(나는 / 당신은 / 그는 / 그녀는 / 그것은 / 우리는 / 당신들은 / 그들은 무엇을 하고 있습니까?)				(당신은 / 나는 / 그는 / 그녀는 / 그것은 / 당신들은 / 우리는 / 그들은 마시고 있습니다.)		

Who Question			Answer		
Who	is	running?	Amy	is	running.
			The children	are	running.
(누가 달리고 있습니까?)			(에이미가 / 아이들이 달리고 있습니다.)		

A **Read, match, and write.**

What

_____What_____ is she doing? She is sleeping.

_____ is driving a car? Dad is driving a car.

_____ are they doing? They are running.

Who

_____ is riding a bike? Amy is riding a bike.

B Look and write.

	climb	walk	swim	write	sing
Diana					✓
Tom and Sue		✓			
Mr. Johnson				✓	
The monkey	✓				
You			✓		

1 What is Diana doing?　　　　➡　_She is singing._

2 What are you doing?　　　　➡　_____

3 What are Tom and Sue doing?　➡　_____

4 Who is writing?　　　　　　➡　_____

5 Who is climbing?　　　　　➡　_____

C Look and write.

1 Peter Pan

2 the seven dwarfs

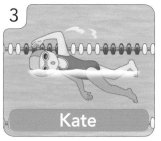
3 Kate

4 you

1 Who ___is flying_____? Peter Pan is flying.

2 What _____? They are working.

3 Who _____? Kate is swimming.

4 What _____? We are riding bikes.

D Read and unscramble.

1 are | doing? | What | you

→ What are you doing?

2 an email? | Who | writing | is

→ _____

3 the cat | is | doing? | What

→ _____

4 is | driving | Who | a car?

→ _____

5 your parents | doing? | are | What

→ _____

E Read and correct.

1 Q Who are they doing? → What are they doing?

   A They are play baseball. → They are playing baseball.

2 Q What is she do? → _____

   A She studying is. → _____

3 Q What is watching TV? → _____

   A Linda watching TV. → _____

4 Q Who is listen to music? → _____

   A Tom are listening to music. → _____

A Read and write.

1 hit
   - I ___am___ ___hitting___ a ball.
   - He _____ _____ a tree.

2 play
   - They _____ _____ soccer.
   - She _____ _____ the piano.

3 ride
   - We _____ _____ bikes.
   - You _____ _____ a horse.

4 go
   - The students _____ _____ to the park.
   - My mom _____ _____ to the market.

B Look, read, and write.

1 Julie is playing a computer game.

   She ___isn't___ ___writing___ an email.

write

2 The children are dancing.

   They _____ _____ TV.

watch

3 The penguins are walking on the ice.

   They _____ _____ in the water.

swim

4 My father is reading a newspaper.

   He _____ _____ to music.

listen

C **Look and write.**

1
_____Are_____ the birds _____flying_____?

No, _____they_____ _____aren't_____.

2
_____ she _____ a bike?

Yes, _____ _____.

3
_____ the children _____?

No, _____ _____.

4
_____ you _____ on the bench?

Yes, _____ _____.

fly ride dance sit

D **Read, circle, and write.**

1 _____What_____ is she doing?

   ⓐ Who   ⓑ What   ⓒ Does

2 What are they _____?

   ⓐ does   ⓑ do   ⓒ doing

3 Who _____ running?

   ⓐ is   ⓑ are   ⓒ am

4 _____ is the bear doing? It is _____.

   ⓐ What, dancing   ⓑ Who, dancing   ⓒ What, dances

5 Who is _____ a letter? Jessie _____ writing a letter.

   ⓐ writes, is   ⓑ writing, write   ⓒ writing, is

Comparatives

GRAMMAR PoINT

형용사의 비교급

● 형용사의 비교급은 두 개의 대상을 비교할 때 사용하며, 비교급 문장 형식은 형용사의 비교급 + than으로, than
다음에는 비교하는 대상을 써서 '~보다 더~하다'라고 해석합니다. 형용사의 비교급을 만드는 방법은 다음과 같습니다.
① 대부분의 1음절 형용사의 경우 형용사 뒤에 –er을 붙입니다.
② –e로 끝나는 형용사는 뒤에는 –r을 붙입니다.
③ 형용사가 자음 + y로 끝나는 경우 y를 i로 고치고 –er을 붙입니다.
④ 형용사가 단모음 + 단자음으로 끝나는 경우 마지막 자음을 하나 더 쓰고 –er을 붙입니다.
⑤ 2음절 이상의 형용사는 앞에 more를 붙입니다.

+ -er	long → longer (더 긴), fast → faster (더 빠른), short → shorter (더 짧은)
+ -r	large → larger (더 큰), nice → nicer (더 좋은), cute → cuter (더 귀여운)
y → i + -er	pretty → prettier (더 예쁜), happy → happier (더 행복한), easy → easier (더 쉬운)
double consonant + -er	big → bigger (더 큰), hot → hotter (더 더운), fat → fatter (더 뚱뚱한)
more + adjective	beautiful → more beautiful (더 아름다운), expensive → more expensive (더 비싼), difficult → more difficult (더 어려운)

A Read and write.

Adjectives	Comparatives	Adjectives	Comparatives
fast	faster		nicer
	longer	big	
pretty			happier
	hotter	large	
beautiful		expensive	

B **Look, circle, and write.**

1  2  3  4

1 (big)/ small   The elephant is ___bigger than___ the mouse.

2 clean / dirty   The skirt is _____ the pants.

3 slow / fast   The turtle is _____ the rabbit.

4 cheap / expensive   The pink hat is _____ the yellow hat.

C **Look and write.**

Name	Age (Year)	Weight (Kg)	Height (Cm)
Mia	12	40	155
Joe	9	28	145
Sandy	10	35	150
Harry	15	45	162

1 (Age) Mia is ___older than___ Sandy.

2 (Weight) Sandy is _____ Joe.

3 (Height) Harry is _____ Mia.

4 (Age) Joe is _____ Sandy.

5 (Weight) Mia is _____ Harry.

6 (Height) Sandy is _____ Mia.

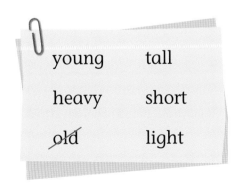

young   tall

heavy   short

old   light

D **Read and unscramble.**

1 [the Yellow River.] [than] [longer] [The Nile is]

→ <u> The Nile is longer than the Yellow River.   </u>

2 [larger] [China is] [Japan.] [than]

→ <u>   </u>

3 [math.] [easier] [than] [English is]

→ <u>   </u>

4 [than] [winter.] [hotter] [Summer is]

→ <u>   </u>

5 [more difficult] [Math is] [than] [English.]

→ <u>   </u>

6 [than] [a flower.] [Amy is] [more beautiful]

→ <u>   </u>

E **Read and correct.**

1 Lisa is prettyer than Amy. → <u> Lisa is prettier than Amy.   </u>

2 English is easy than math. → <u>   </u>

3 The train is longer the car. → <u>   </u>

4 Summer is hoter than spring. → <u>   </u>

5 The car is expensive than the bike. → <u>   </u>

6 The giraffe is taller the monkey. → <u>   </u>

Superlatives

GRAMMAR POINT

형용사의 최상급

- 형용사의 최상급은 세 개 이상의 대상을 비교할 때 사용하며, '가장 ~한'의 의미로 형용사의 최상급 앞에는 항상 정관사 the를 씁니다. 형용사의 최상급을 만드는 방법은 다음과 같습니다.
  ① 대부분의 1음절 형용사의 경우 형용사 뒤에 –est를 붙입니다.
  ② –e로 끝나는 형용사 뒤에는 –st을 붙입니다.
  ③ 형용사가 자음 + y로 끝나는 경우 y를 i로 고치고 –est를 붙입니다.
  ④ 형용사가 단모음 + 단자음으로 끝나는 경우 마지막 자음을 하나 더 쓰고 –est를 붙입니다.
  ⑤ 2음절 이상의 형용사는 앞에 most를 붙입니다.

+ -est	long → longest (가장 긴), fast → fastest (가장 빠른), short → shortest (가장 짧은)
+ -st	large → largest (가장 큰), nice → nicest (가장 멋진), cute → cutest (가장 귀여운)
y → i + -est	pretty → prettiest (가장 예쁜), happy → happiest (가장 행복한), easy → easiest (가장 쉬운)
double consonant + -est	big → biggest (가장 큰), hot → hottest (가장 더운), fat → fattest (가장 뚱뚱한)
most + adjective	beautiful → most beautiful (가장 아름다운), expensive → most expensive (가장 비싼), difficult → most difficult (가장 어려운)

A Read and write.

1 fast → the ___fastest___

2 hot → the _____

3 easy → the _____

4 nice → the _____

5 short → the _____

6 heavy → the _____

7 pretty → the _____

8 expensive → the _____

9 fat → the _____

10 beautiful → the _____

B Look and write.

1

Suzy is ___taller than___ Kelly.

Tom is ___the tallest___ student.

2

Maxie is _____ Cony.

Buster is _____ dog.

3

Snow White is _____ Fiona.

Cinderella is _____ woman.

big
ta̶l̶l̶
beautiful

C Look and write.

Pet	Weight (Kg)	Length (Cm)	Price ($)
Hamster	0.1	10	7.00
Rabbit	4.0	50	35.00
Turtle	1.5	25	40.00

1 (Weight) The hamster is ___the lightest___ pet.

2 (Length) The rabbit is _____ pet.

3 (Price) The turtle is _____ pet.

4 (Weight) The rabbit is _____ pet.

5 (Length) The hamster is _____ pet.

6 (Price) The hamster is _____ pet.

heavy

li̶g̶h̶t̶

long

short

expensive

cheap

D Read and unscramble.

1 | river. | The Nile is | the | longest |

→ <u>The Nile is the longest river.</u>

2 | the | country. | biggest | Russia is |

→ _____

3 | boy. | the most | Sam is | handsome |

→ _____

4 | Cinderella is | prettiest | woman. | the |

→ _____

5 | The blue whale is | heaviest | the | animal. |

→ _____

6 | the | Mt. Everest is | moutain. | highest |

→ _____

E Read and correct.

1 English is the easyest class. → <u>English is the easiest class.</u>

2 Summer is hottest season. → _____

3 The cheetah is the fast animal. → _____

4 Tom is the most heavy boy. → _____

5 Math is the difficultest class. → _____

6 The elephant is largest animal. → _____

Imperatives / Let's

GRAMMAR POINT

명령문 (긍정명령문 / 부정명령문)

- 명령문은 상대방에게 어떠한 행동을 지시하거나 명령할 때 사용합니다.
- 긍정명령문은 주어를 생략하고 동사원형으로 시작하며 '~ 해라'라고 해석하고, 부정명령문은 문장의 맨 앞에 있는 동사원형에 Don't를 붙이고 '~ 하지 마라'라고 해석합니다.

청유문

- 청유문은 어떤 일을 제안하거나 권유할 때 사용하며, Let's + 동사원형의 형태를 사용합니다.
- 청유문은 '함께 ~하자'라고 해석합니다.

Imperatives (명령문)		Let's (청유문)
Do (Affirmative) (긍정명령문)	**Don't (Negative)** (부정명령문)	
Wash your hands. (손을 씻으세요.) Clean your room. (방을 청소하세요.) Turn on the radio. (라디오를 켜세요.)	Don't play the piano. (피아노를 치지 마세요.) Don't close the window. (창문을 닫지 마세요.) Don't bring your umbrella. (우산을 가져가지 마세요.)	Let's study English. (영어를 공부하자.) Let's make a circle. (원을 만들자.) Let's play baseball. (야구를 하자.)

A Read, circle, and write.

1 (Close) | Closes   _____Close_____ the window.

2 Is | Be   _____ quiet, please.

3 Don't | Not   _____ bring your jacket.

4 Don't   sleep | sleeps   _____ in class.

5 Do | Does   _____ your homework.

6 Let's | Lets   _____ make a snowman.

7 Let's   study | studying   _____ English.

B Read and change.

1 Play computer games. ➡ <u>Don't play computer games.</u>

2 Take off your shoes. ➡ _____

3 Touch your nose. ➡ _____

4 Close the window. ➡ _____

5 Sit on the bench. ➡ _____

6 Bring your umbrella. ➡ _____

C Look, choose, and write.

> Let's make a snowman. Be quiet, please. ~~Don't play the piano.~~
> Don't open the door. Let's turn on the light. Wash your hands.

1

<u>Don't play the piano.</u>

2

_____

3

_____

4

_____

5

_____

6

_____

D Read and unscramble.

1 [jacket.] [your] [Bring]

➜ _Bring your jacket._

2 [your] [hands.] [Wash]

➜ _____

3 [the bench.] [on] [Don't] [sit]

➜ _____

4 [be] [for school.] [Don't] [late]

➜ _____

5 [Let's] [the light.] [turn on]

➜ _____

6 [make] [a] [Let's] [snowman.]

➜ _____

E Read and correct.

1 Turns on the radio. ➜ _Turn on the radio._

2 Don't opens the window. ➜ _____

3 Does your homework. ➜ _____

4 Doesn't use a cell phone. ➜ _____

5 Let go swimming. ➜ _____

6 Let's has a race. ➜ _____

Can/May/Should

GRAMMAR POINT

조동사

● 조동사는 본동사 앞에 위치하여 본동사로 하여금 능력, 허락, 충고나 권유 등의 의미를 갖게하며, 뒤에는 본동사의 원형이 옵니다.
  • **Can**: 본동사로 하여금 능력의 의미를 갖게 하며, '～ 할 수 있다'로 해석합니다.
  • **Can / May**: 본동사로 하여금 허락의 의미를 갖게 하며, '～ 해도 된다'로 해석합니다.
  • **Should**: 본동사로 하여금 충고나 권유의 의미를 갖게 하며, '～ 해야 한다'로 해석합니다.

● 조동사의 부정형은 조동사 뒤에 not을 붙이며, 줄여서 can not → can't, should not → shouldn't를 사용하기도 하나, may not은 축약형이 없습니다.

Can Ability (능력)	I can dance. (나는 춤을 출 수 있습니다.) I can't dance. (나는 춤을 출 수 없습니다.) Can you dance? (당신은 춤을 출 수 있습니까?) Yes, I can. / No, I can't.
Can / May Permission (허락)	You can (may) watch TV. (당신은 TV를 봐도 됩니다.) / You can't (may not) sit down. (당신은 앉으면 안됩니다.) Can (May) I come in? (들어가도 될까요?) Yes, you can (may). / No, you can't (may not).
Should Advice (충고 / 권유)	You should brush your teeth. (당신은 이를 닦아야 합니다.) You shouldn't watch TV. (당신은 TV를 보면 안됩니다.)

A Write *Can* for ability and *May* for permission.

1 ___Can___ the birds fly?

2 ___May___ I drink some milk?

3 _____ you speak English?

4 _____ the frog jump high?

5 _____ I turn off the radio?

6 _____ I use your computer?

7 _____ I borrow your book?

8 _____ the chicken fly?

B **Read and write *should* or *shouldn't*.**

1 I have a cold. I ___should___ ___see___ a doctor.

2 We _____ _____ too much TV.

3 She _____ _____ her teeth.

4 It is rainy. You _____ _____ your umbrella.

5 You _____ _____ the piano at night.

6 You _____ _____ your homework.

brush

watch

do

bring

play

see

C **Look and write.**

1

Can the frog fly?

___No, it cant.___ It can jump.

2

May I borrow your book?

_____ Here you are.

3

Can I open the window?

_____ It is hot.

4

May I sit down?

_____ It is wet.

5

Your room is messy.

You _____ clean your room.

6

Everyone is sleeping.

You _____ play the piano.

D Read and unscramble.

1 [I] [the window?] [May] [open]

   → <u>May I open the window?</u>

2 [your hands.] [should] [You] [wash]

   → _____

3 [She] [the piano.] [can't] [play]

   → _____

4 [sit down.] [You] [not] [may]

   → _____

5 [Can] [your book?] [I] [borrow]

   → _____

6 [junk food.] [eat] [You] [shouldn't]

   → _____

E Read and correct.

1 The frog can't flies.   → <u>The frog can't fly.</u>

2 May I borrows your eraser?   → _____

3 Can I drinks some water?   → _____

4 May I come in? <u>No, you mayn't.</u> → _____

5 You should brushes your teeth. → _____

6 You not should watch TV.   → _____

Units 17-20

A Read and write.

	Adjectives	Comparatives	Superlatives
1	easy	easier	the _____easiest_____
2	large		the _____
3	long		the _____
4	difficult		the _____
5	fat		the _____
6	beautiful		the _____
7	pretty		the _____

B Read and write.

1 Venus is ____the hottest____ planet.
　　　　　　　　hot

2 The cheetah is ____faster than____ the zebra.
　　　　　　　　　　fast

3 Mt. Everest is _____ moutain.
　　　　　　　　　　high

4 Peter is _____ Tom.
　　　　　　　fat

5 Jane is _____ girl in the class.
　　　　　　　tall

6 Fishing is _____ camping.
　　　　　　　　interesting

7 The blue whale is _____ animal in the world.
　　　　　　　　　　heavy

8 The elephant is _____ the tiger.
　　　　　　　　　large

C Look, choose, and write.

1 It is rainy. _Close the window._

2 Everyone is sleeping. _____

3 It is snowing. _____

4 You have a cold. _____

Let's make a snowman.   Don't play the piano.
Don't play outside.   ~~Close the window.~~

D Read, circle, and write.

1 A penguin ____can't____ fly. It ____can____ swim.

   ⓐ can, may   ⓑ can't, can   ⓒ may not, may

2 Can I use your cell phone? Yes, you _____.

   ⓐ can   ⓑ can't   ⓒ may

3 May I watch TV? No, you _____.

   ⓐ aren't   ⓑ may not   ⓒ can't

4 You _____ sleep in class.

   ⓐ are   ⓑ should   ⓒ shouldn't

5 You are sick. You _____ see a doctor.

   ⓐ shouldn't   ⓑ should   ⓒ aren't

Prepositions of Place

GRAMMAR PoInT

장소를 나타내는 전치사

● 장소를 나타내는 전치사는 사람이나 사물이 있는 곳을 나타낼 때 사용하며 명사 앞에 위치합니다.

● 장소를 나타내는 전치사에는 in, on, under, in front of, behind, next to 등이 있습니다.

● Where은 장소를 물을 때 사용하는 의문사로 문장의 맨 앞에 오며, '~이 어디에'라고 해석합니다.

in (~ 안에)	on (~ 위에)	under (~ 아래에)

in front of (~ 앞에)	behind (~ 뒤에)	next to (~ 옆에)

A Look and match.

1  •   • The rabbits are next to the tree.

2  •   • The rabbit is under the hat.

3  •   • The rabbits are behind the tree.

4  •   • The rabbit is in the hat.

B Look and write.

1

The bear is ____on____ the ball.

2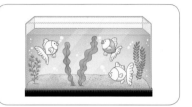

The clock is _____ the TV.

3

The fish are _____ the fish tank.

4

The rabbit is _____ the hat.

5

The girl is _____ the door.

6

The balls are _____ the box.

C Look and correct.

1

The flowers are behind the vase.
→ _The flowers are in the vase._____

2

The socks are in the sofa.
→ _____

3

The car is next to the house.
→ _____

4

The slippers are in front of the bed.
→ _____

D Read and unscramble.

1 | in | is | the drawer. | My watch |

→ <u>My watch is in the drawer.</u>

2 | next to | are | The bats | the door. |

→ _____

3 | The chairs | the table. | are | behind |

→ _____

4 | the sofa. | The cat | is | on |

→ _____

5 | My father | the car. | in front of | is |

→ _____

E Read and write.

1 | Where / the pencils | | on the desk |

→ <u>Where are the pencils?</u>   <u>They are on the desk.</u>

2 | Where / the socks | | under the sofa |

→ _____   _____

3 | Where / the dog | | behind the door |

→ _____   _____

4 | Where / the robots | | next to the box |

→ _____   _____

5 | Where / the car | | in front of the house |

→ _____   _____

Prepositions of Time

GRAMMAR POINT

시간을 나타내는 전치사

- 시간을 나타내는 전치사는 시점이나 때를 나타낼 때 사용하여 명사 앞에 위치합니다.
- 시간을 나타내는 전치사에는 at, on, in 등이 있으며, 시간, 정오, 밤 등의 앞에는 at을 사용하고, 날짜, 요일 등의 앞에는 on을 사용하며, 월, 계절, 오전, 오후, 저녁 등의 앞에는 in을 사용합니다.
- When은 시간을 물을 때 사용하는 의문사로 문장의 맨 앞에 오며, '~이 언제인지'라고 해석합니다.

at + time	on + day / date	in + month / season
at 4 o'clock (4시 정각에) at 7:30　　(7시 30분에) at noon　　(정오에)	on Monday (월요일에) on Sundays (일요일마다) on May 5　　(5월 5일에)	in July　　　(7월에) in winter　　(겨울에) in the morning (아침에)

A **Look and write.**

> at　　　　on　　　　in

1

___on__ Monday

2

_____ 7 o'clock

3

_____ January

4

_____ night

5

_____ August 10

6

_____ winter

B **Read and write.**

1 My father goes fishing __on__ Saturdays.

2 She doesn't play the piano _____ night.

3 It is warm _____ spring.

4 My birthday is _____ Tuesday.

5 We have dinner _____ 7 o'clock.

6 Christmas is _____ December 25.

7 I go to sleep _____ 9:30.

8 Halloween is _____ October.

at

on

in

C **Read and write.**

1 When is Tom's birthday?

   It is __on__ __Tuesday__ .

2 When is English class?

   It is _____ _____.

3 When is summer vacation?

   It is _____ _____.

4 When is the Christmas party?

   It is _____ _____.

Schedule

Tom's Birthday
Tuesday

Summer Vacation
August

Christmas Party
December 24

English Class
10:30

D **Read and unscramble.**

1 | gets up | 6 o'clock. | She | at |

→ <u>She gets up at 6 o'clock.</u>

2 | in | cold | It is | winter. |

→ _____

3 | on | a test | Monday. | I have |

→ _____

4 | October. | Halloween | is | in |

→ _____

5 | on | April 5. | is | My birthday |

→ _____

6 | noon. | We have | at | lunch |

→ _____

E **Read and correct.**

1 I get up on 7 o'clock. → <u>I get up at 7 o'clock.</u>

2 We go swimming in Friday. → _____

3 Tom's birthday is at January. → _____

4 Don't play the piano in night. → _____

5 Christmas is at December 25. → _____

6 It is hot on summer. → _____

There Is / There Isn't / Is There …?

GRAMMAR POINT

There Is 구문

- 사람이나 사물이 있다고 얘기할 때, There is/are 구문을 사용하며, There is 다음에는 단수명사나 셀 수 없는 명사가 오고, There are 다음에는 복수명사가 옵니다.
- There is/are 구문의 부정문은 is/are 뒤에 not을 붙여 만들며 줄여서 There isn't/aren't로 씁니다.
- There is/are 구문의 의문문은 is/are와 There의 위치를 바꾸어 Is there …?/Are there …?로 만들고, 대답은 Yes나 No로 합니다.
- some과 any는 복수명사 또는 셀 수 없는 명사와 함께 사용하며, some은 긍정문에, any는 부정문과 의문문에 사용합니다.

	Countable Noun	Uncountable Noun
Affirmative (긍정문)	There is **an apple**. (사과가 한 개 있습니다.) There are **two apples**. (사과가 두 개 있습니다.) There are **some apples**. (사과가 몇 개 있습니다.)	There is **some milk**. (약간의 우유가 있습니다.)
Negative (부정문)	There isn't **an apple**. (사과 한 개가 없습니다.) There aren't **any apples**. (사과가 없습니다.)	There isn't **any milk**. (우유가 없습니다.)
Question (의문문)	Is there **an apple**? (사과가 한 개 있습니까?) **Yes**, there is. / **No**, there isn't. Are there **any apples**? (사과가 있습니까?) **Yes**, there are. / **No**, there aren't.	Is there **any milk**? (우유가 있습니까?) **Yes**, there is. / **No**, there isn't.

A Read and write *is* or *are*.

1 There ____is____ a watch.

2 There _____ some money.

3 There _____ not any pencils.

4 There _____ not any butter.

5 There _____ some books.

6 There _____ not an orange.

7 _____ there any homework?

8 _____ there any eggs?

B **Look, choose, and write.**

| There is | There are | There isn't | There aren't |

1 ___There are___ some eggs.

2 _____ three fish.

3 _____ some bread.

4 _____ any cheese.

5 _____ some ice cream.

6 _____ any potatoes.

7 _____ a watermelon.

8 _____ any milk.

C **Read and write.**

1 [a balloon] → ___Is there a balloon___ ? No, there isn't.

2 [toys] → _____ ? Yes, there are.

3 [bread] → _____ ? Yes, there is.

4 [cars] → _____ ? No, there aren't.

5 [cheese] → _____ ? No, there isn't.

6 [an igloo] → _____ ? Yes, there is.

D Read and unscramble.

1　| is | There | alligator. | an |

→ <u>There is an alligator.</u>

2　| some | chocolate. | There | is |

→ _____

3　| chairs. | aren't | any | There |

→ _____

4　| any | There | butter. | isn't |

→ _____

5　| there | Are | apples? | any |

→ _____

6　| Is | any | there | water? |

→ _____

E Read and correct.

1 There aren't any bread.　→ <u>There isn't any bread.</u>

2 There is some notebooks.　→ _____

3 There are some ice cream.　→ _____

4 There isn't any pencils.　→ _____

5 Are there some umbrellas?　→ _____

6 Are there any butter?　→ _____

What ...! How ...!

GRAMMAR PoINT

감탄문

- 감탄문은 놀람, 기쁨 등의 감정을 나타낼 때 사용합니다.
- 감탄문은 What 또는 How로 시작하며, '정말 ~구나!'라로 해석합니다.
- What으로 시작하는 감탄문은 What + a / an + 형용사 + 명사 + (주어 + 동사)!의 어순이며, 복수명사일 경우 a나 an은 쓰지 않습니다. 이 때 뒤에 있는 주어 + 동사는 생략이 가능합니다.
- How로 시작하는 감탄문은 How + 형용사 + (주어 + 동사)!의 어순이며, 뒤에 있는 주어 + 동사는 생략이 가능합니다.

Exclamations		
What + a / an + adjective + noun + (S + V)!	**What + adjective + plural noun + (S + V)!**	**How + adjective + (S + V)!**
What a nice hat (it is)! (정말 멋진 모자구나!) What a beautiful girl (she is)! (정말 아름다운 소녀구나!) What an ugly boy (he is)! (정말 못생긴 소년이구나!)	What pretty flowers (they are)! (정말 예쁜 꽃들이구나!) What tall boys (they are)! (정말 키가 큰 소년들이구나!) What big houses (they are)! (정말 큰 집들이구나!)	How expensive (it is)! (정말 비싸구나!) How smart (she is)! (정말 똑똑하구나!) How sweet (they are)! (정말 달콤하구나!)

A Read, circle, and write.

1 (What) I How   ____What____ a beautiful flower!

2 What I How   _____ interesting!

3 What I How   _____ tall buildings!

4 What I How   _____ fast!

5 What I How   _____ an ugly frog!

6 What I How   _____ handsome!

B **Look and write.**

cute	strong	smart	fast
~~beautiful~~	big	dirty	expensive

1

What a ___beautiful___ flower it is!

= How ___beautiful___ it is!

2

What a _____ train it is!

= How _____ it is!

3

What _____ boys they are!

= How _____ they are!

4

What an _____ camera it is!

= How _____ it is!

5

What a _____ girl she is!

= How _____ she is!

6

What _____ students they are!

= How _____ they are!

7

What a _____ house it is!

= How _____ it is!

8

What _____ shoes they are!

= How _____ they are!

C **Look and write.**

1  It is a fast airplane. ➡ <u>What a fast airplane!</u>

2  He is strong. ➡ <u>How strong!</u>

3  She is a cute girl. ➡ _____

4  It is an ugly frog. ➡ _____

5  They are big. ➡ _____

D **Read and correct.**

1 Pretty how she is! ➡ <u>How pretty she is!</u>

2 What an beautiful flower! ➡ _____

3 How an interesting game! ➡ _____

4 What cheap they are! ➡ _____

5 How tall buildings! ➡ _____

6 What old an house! ➡ _____

A Look and write the correct number.

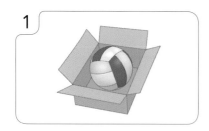

1 The ball is _①_ the box.

2 The ball is ____ the box.

3 The ball is ____ the box.

4 The balls are ____ the box.

5 The balls are ____ the box.

6 The balls are ____ the box.

① in   ② on   ③ in front of   ④ next to   ⑤ under   ⑥ behind

B Read and write.

1 When is the midterm exam?

  It is _on_ _May 9_ .

2 When is the class meeting?

  It is ____ _____ .

3 When is the school trip?

  It is ____ _____ .

4 When is the computer class?

  It is ____ _____ .

Schedule

School Trip
April

Computer Class
Friday

Midterm Exam
May 9

Class Meeting
2:00

C Read, circle, and write.

1 There _____is_____ some bread.

    ⓐ is   ⓑ are   ⓒ be

2 There _____ any toys.

    ⓐ are   ⓑ aren't   ⓒ isn't

3 There _____ an elephant.

    ⓐ are   ⓑ be   ⓒ isn't

4 There _____ any water.

    ⓐ is   ⓑ are   ⓒ isn't

5 _____ there any pencils? No, they _____.

    ⓐ Are, are   ⓑ Are, aren't   ⓒ Is, isn't

6 _____ there any cheese? Yes, there _____.

    ⓐ Is, is   ⓑ Are, are   ⓒ Is, are

D Read, circle, and write.

1 ___What___ a pretty house!

    ⓐ Who   ⓑ What   ⓒ How

2 _____ beautiful she is!

    ⓐ Who   ⓑ What   ⓒ How

3 _____ tall buildings!

    ⓐ What   ⓑ How   ⓒ When

4 What _____ ugly frog!

    ⓐ a   ⓑ an   ⓒ be

5 How _____ fast it is!

    ⓐ can   ⓑ an   ⓒ X

Written by E2K
Illustrated by Younga Choi

First published September 2012
5th printing January 2023

Publisher: Kyudo Chung
Editorial Manager: Mija Cho
Editors: Mikyoung Kim, Jungwon Min, Genie Jeong
Designers: Eunhee Lee, D#

Published and distributed by
Happy House, an imprint of DARAKWON, Inc.
Darakwon Bldg., 211 Munbal-ro, Paju-si, Gyeonggi-do, 10881, Republic of Korea
Tel: 82-2-736-2031(Ext.250) **Fax:** 82-2-732-2037 **Hompage:** www.ihappyhouse.co.kr

ISBN: 978-89-6653-077-9 63740
Price: ₩7,000

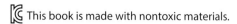 This book is made with nontoxic materials.